10 Critical Success Answers for Small Business Enterprises.

DAVID MUGUN

DEDICATION

To the businessperson who leaves nothing to chance.

CONTENTS

Acknowledgments   i

1   When to let go of employment   7

2   Setting up shop from scratch or, when expanding an existing outfit to a new environment   11

3   Cross border expansion   15

4   Problems faced by Small Business Enterprises   21

5   The pitfalls of Small Business Enterprises   25

6   The Bank   29

7   An Excellent Product   34

8   Selling to the rich   37

9   Branding   43

10 Personal Branding   49

Foot Notes   52

ACKNOWLEDGMENTS

To Almighty God, for the strength, insights and concentration to have this project accomplished.

To every experience and advice that favoured the writing of this book, I owe a lot.

To everyone who has taught me something positive, given me a chance to work for you or work with you, this book is a reflection of your positive inspiration.

To my Publishers, this would not be possible without your support. I am most grateful.

1

WHEN TO LET GO OF EMPLOYMENT.

The big question: When does it make sense to be in business vis-a-vis full time employment?

Both being in employment and doing business, brings success but in different ways.

People on either side are comfortable with their objectives in life until we examine the differences that make a case for self-employment.

Those who have had an opportunity to make a transition from employment to business or vice versa will agree with this chapter. If you have not had the chance, then here is some good advice.

Before I proceed, I want to state that self-employment rides on requisite skills and that I am not implying that everybody becomes an entrepreneur so please trust what your calling is.

Both the employed and the self-employed pay taxes and at this point I want to borrow from Robert Kiyosaki the author of the best seller "Rich Dad poor Dad."

In chapter five, under the topic, "The history of Taxes and the power of corporations" he makes a clear case for self-employment. He discusses how taxation came to be in both the USA and England.[1]

Originally, citizens paid taxes solely to finance wars.

In America, taxes were levied to pay for the civil war from 1861 to '65 while in Britain taxes were levied in the fight against Napoleon in 1799 to 1816. Later on, the Government convinced the masses that only the rich would pay taxes. Therefore, with song, dance and fanfare, they passed the vote unanimously.

Government appetite for more money later cut short the party when the poor became taxpayers. As the poor waited for a pay cheque monthly that was net of tax, the rich styled up and set up corporations, which legally were, and still are allowed to first spend then pay taxes unlike the employed.

The self-employed have a freer hand in putting to use the money they generate before the government gets its bit. Independent contractors pay withholding tax at a lower rate than Pay as You Earn tax, say at 5% and can claim it depending on the level of expenses when they submit their returns.

Do the taxation arithmetic of an employee earning Kes. One hundred thousand per month and that of a consultant making the same amount monthly. There you go! Remember that the trade off is additional responsibility.

Employers normally splash a bouquet of benefits to valued employees with the obvious intention of retaining good talent. This has different responses from the intended targets. Some will feel fulfilled and stay motivated while others will react in the opposite direction.

Making a case for self-employment is a personal and calculated decision and never the product of gut feel. Recently, I met an old-time friend who has since moved on to self-employment. The turning point was courtesy of an incentive for a holiday abroad with his family on an all expenses paid basis.

He reasoned out that, his employer's gesture had a direct relationship to his efforts. He declined the holiday and set up his own company. Six months down the road, he made the trip together with his family. This is a rare case but the reality of switching roles and succeeding within a short span of time exists.

If your answers to the following are YES, then you are ready and more likely to succeed in business.

1. Do you have the necessary experience and qualifications to undertake the business of your choice?

2. Do you have your plan written out?

3. Do you have your research right?

4. Do you have support from your immediate family regarding going it alone?

5. Do you have enough contacts to support you in the event that you switch? Have you sounded some of your potential targets?

6. Do you have sufficient finances or well-researched sources of the same?

7. Do you have a good management information system that you will install?

8. Will your switch earn you more money than when you are in employment?

9. Will you have a sober and experienced board that can see you through all the way?

10. Do you have the required energy levels?

11. Do you mind a lower quality life until you stabilize?

If your answers to the questions above, are clearly unsettling then I advice that you remain in the comfort of your present job or occupation.

2

SETTING UP SHOP FROM SCRATCH OR EXPANDING AN EXISITING OUTFIT TO A NEW ENVIRONMENT.

The big Question: What do I need to know when setting up a completely new business or when expanding an existing business in a new environment?

New things come with a package. A new day, brings a breath of fresh air, bursts of energy and the opportunity to do better than yesterday. The new day, also carries with it new experiences of mixed luck, introduces the young into the world and provides a platform for the old to pass down knowledge.

Every day is a new day for someone or something and our ever-increasing population and technology advancements justify business expansion. As we know it, expansion in to new territories has its fair share of challenges and opportunities. What kind of reception, should the executive tasked with setting up a new business expect and what kind of attitude enables him to thrive? Does he make it feel like Christmas came early?

Let us set off on a positive note and discuss what the new Santa Claus brings to town.

1. Expansion brings with it employment opportunities. When the required knowledge and skills are locally available and brought on board, this serves as a platform to endear the newcomer to the host town or the community residents as they get to identify with it through the locals absorbed into service.

This in turn further aids market penetration when the champions are well known. Acceptability has a domino effect and can set you on a continuous business based door opening frenzy.

2. Being new makes you the point of focus and especially when organized to give a positive outlook, it provides you with the opportunity to be exciting and known everywhere.

This is good for business because it ensures that your investment is on the path to encouraging returns. A badly handled beginning can make you fodder for your competitors.

3. Price cuts by the new comer are often times excusable and may not trigger a price war. Introductory offers serve to create positive attention for you. How you manage this aspect is also critical, as the old boy network in town might swing into action and ensure that you spend more than you had budgeted for.

4. A new business set up or expansion to new territory, provides us with opportunities to do things right. It eliminates models riddled with prejudice and free of negative baggage. New operations sometimes prove to be the cradle of new business-wide innovative cultures.

5. The experience of setting up a business is a valuable life-long experience for the responsible executive. This experience in most cases separates colleagues at the same level, and facilitates faster promotions to the top when in employment and later on can prove beneficial should one, be caught by the entrepreneurial bug. For the entrepreneur, such experiences serve to redouble

personal resolve and company value, which in turn yields greater results.

6. Another positive, is that a new entrant, always makes the existing competitors to pull up their socks so that customers do not abandon them in the wake of new standards. This state, benefits all consumers and the credit of the new improvements goes to the new kid on the block.

Early positive results position the new outfit as a thought-leader and hence an opinion leader. This is critical as it makes the public trust your products as you exude confidence.

Setting up late, provides you with the opportunity to learn from everyone's mistakes. This ensures that you have higher chances of succeeding and catching up because of no need to reinvent the wheel. If not careful, the old boy network can use you to do all the research for someone else to use hence minimizing your impact.

There is a flipside to being the new kid on the block.

1. It is very possible to misread your early results strategy and think that success has come faster than expected but in reality, you are building a poor portfolio by gathering all the trash and rejects in town. You may delight your competition by incepting loan defaulters, bad debtors, reputation-poor busybodies and the market lunatic. Remember that what weakens you strengthens your competitors.

2. Stemming from point one above is the unfortunate possibility, of putting good money after bad efforts by having an inexperienced person to open your new operation.

Inexperience can either take the form of being very new in a new environment or having a leader with questionable abilities setting up the business. You become a see-through and everyone can tell when you are walking into the fire.

3. You risk becoming the experiment of a more established competitor if, they infiltrate your recruitment process or overall

strategy. They can plant spies and haemorrhage your operation. A hostile old boy network can keep you at bay and cost you good opportunities.

4. It pays to plan well in order to mitigate negative experiences long before you set foot to new grounds.

3

CROSS BORDER EXPANSION

The big question: What do I need to have in mind when expanding across country borders?

You need business etiquette and an understanding of the market culture.

Why do I need these factors?

The business world today is no longer round and as difficult to navigate. If anything, it got flattened by technology, trade agreements, readily available and abundant expertise, bilinguals, political policy shifts, infrastructure to name but a few.

What we have is a global village. In Kenya today, someone, could be planning or is implementing regional expansion perhaps across shared borders in to Uganda, Tanzania, Rwanda, Burundi, Ethiopia, Southern Sudan and Somalia. Let us use the South African experience in Kenya to further our answer.

With the end of Apartheid in South Africa, Global economic sanctions got relaxed. The business community in South Africa declared the rest of Africa as its extended back yard and marched northwards conquering every market on the way.

We saw the South Africans who ventured into Kenya in the '90s. They had a low success rate despite having sufficient amounts of money and the expertise necessary for the various ventures that they set up.

Metro cash and carry, Cook International (biscuits) and many others came in and ended just as a football match does. Physical energy and money spent on tickets to valuable lessons. They continued to fall by the wayside until later on when the approach changed.

As recently, as two years ago, a South African firm with excellent credentials and a mood to expand showed up at the doorsteps of an investment bank hitherto, one of the oldest stock broking houses in Kenya.

They demanded to speak to the owners. The name of the firm seemed to suggest that it is white owned. To their amazement, the owners were black indigenous Kenyans who were not holding brief for white owners because of a black empowerment program as is the case down south.[2] they were shocked that the firm was not for sale but was also keen on setting up in South Africa.

Therefore, to succeed where their compatriots had failed earlier, the South Africans began to either get into joint ventures or buy into existing Kenyan companies. They bought into companies that were already stable and by extension; they were buying into an existing culture. Perhaps that is why they approached the stock broking house earlier.

They bought the Pan Africa Insurance Company, Africa Online, more recently a controlling stake in HACO industries and many more. This is common knowledge given that these events received good coverage in the newspapers. So why did this approach work?

Having burned their fingers earlier from a *cut and paste* approach that rode on the belief that Africa's fundamentals were all the same and therefore economic might, mattered most, they very expensively realized that there was much more.

They needed to understand the working culture of Kenya, which so far was unique and different from all the other markets that they had conquered.

Over time, it is gradually easier to change an existing culture and in this case, especially one where its brand is deeply embedded in the market, than to introducing a new one.

The frog analogy works here. The frog's confidence levels in the water are high and so to kill it while in water is difficult, if you threw it into a pot of hot water, it would jump out because it feels the sudden change in temperature. However, if it is resting in a pot full of water, and you heat the pot, the frog remains in its comfort zone and realizes what was happening when it is too late.

When starting from scratch, you save yourself tones of money just by first understanding the business culture of a country. There is a communication principle that states that "Cognitive processes are culturally determined" meaning the way a people think is influenced by established culture.

 Culture requires a set of beliefs, practices, an environment, perceptions, experiences, symbols and a mode of communication to thrive. If you miss these, you miss big time.

So what must we do if we are to expand successfully?

With all your business supporting cases and plans at hand, it is critical to know and understand what our collective perception is in the eyes and minds of our target markets. This way we can tackle obstacles better.

So what is the typical Kenyan like in the eyes of our neighbours?

We are considered as extremely aggressive and thus an immediate threat to the business ventures across our borders. A case in point is in the legal profession. In the spirit of East African cooperation, Kenya has extended an open arm to Uganda and Tanzania for their lawyers to practice law in Kenya but, the two sister countries are reluctant to reciprocate fully partly because of the   perceived aggression and the fact that Kenya has lawyers who outnumber those in Uganda and Tanzania.

Perception is also relative. A few years ago, I attended a conference that had seven countries amongst them Malawi a southern African country with no shared borders with Kenya. The Malawians perceive the Tanzanians as extremely aggressive and in fact, "the Tanzanians own a big market in Malawi and many businesses"... they went on and on about how they view Kenyans as polite businesswise.

In some quarters, Kenyans come out arrogant due to their straight talk. "Can I have" instead of, "May I please have" or "I beg to have" when translated from Swahili.[3] this has been the identifying mark of Kenyans in Tanzania.

Kenyans at times, are judged as somewhat inconsiderate to some with regard to our employment contracts. In two East African countries, and unlike in Kenya, lunch is a big deal. Someone can refuse to sign an employment contract because there is no provision for lunch. From our perspective, this may be ridiculous but it is a system embedded in the work ethic just across and beyond our very borders.

The stereotypes fanned soon after independence have not helped us at all. The ideological differences at the time still form country memory. All these are a cause of friction or annoyance for the ordinary Kenyan. I advise that you exercise emotional intelligence on these issues that have lingered on for over forty years.

It is worth pointing out, that a number of our neighbours have been in Kenya unfortunately because of political instability in their countries. Some of these people would gauge Kenya depending on how they were treated. How they behave here is not necessarily their modus operandi at home.

We now talk freely of our politics and may get tempted to do so while out there and end up in big trouble. It is good to understand the politics of another country for business purposes but not to add it to day-to-day commentaries.

Remember that not all Kenyans have been good ambassadors while in the region. We have heard of stories of our citizens' not fulfilling contracts to the letter, or arrested for unlawful conduct and the like. Depending on whom you will be dealing with, these may be perceptions of you even before you set foot out there.

We are not that bad you may think. However, it is the negative perceptions that one ought to be conscious of, as nobody will give you a medal for our good aspects if anything, becoming an athlete just might get you closer to it because we have renowned athletes.

Language barriers across have ensured that our experiences are equally reduced. Other than Swahili and the languages spoken along common borders, we heavily depend on English, a language that is not widely used outside of Uganda and Tanzania. We may need our schools to teach Amharic[4] and the other widely spoken languages. We must be willing to learn them.

Whereas Somalia is relatively dangerous now, nevertheless substantial business is transacted with Kenya. Should you choose to go there, you must have strong Somali connections to ensure your safety. A visit to Wilson airport may just help shape your thoughts about business in Somalia.

So far, we have dwelt on external perceptions of us. Let us now consider some of the things to expect.

Just like South Africans in the '90s in Kenya, we may misread the cultures out there. Kenyans will no doubt find that the work ethic in all neighbouring countries vary from our own.

One will struggle to make the new outfit work as though it were in Nairobi while the host country employees will keep business style as usual. The gap between the expected culture and the actual culture out there is what determines how good a business manger is, as s/he has to balance reality and results.

You still find out there protectionist employment laws that may have you stuck with an unproductive staff member whom you cannot fire. So getting your recruitment right the first time is critical.

When you travel out there, be clear on the legal limit of money you can hold lest you find yourself in trouble.

The food also varies and may pose a challenge to the very sensitive stomach. Always research on what is readily available. If you are not happy with what is available, Kenyans out there will come in handy in getting you settled.

Cultural and religious beliefs ought to be respected just as you would expect of any visitor.

Consider legal help on lease arrangements as the laws vary from our own.

Would it surprise you that most of the regional perceptions are not at play when doing business away from the region? The Americans love our accent and care less when getting service through a Kenyan based call centre. Far eastern countries supposedly with bigger language and cultural barriers are streaming in for serious business. No one in the region seems to have issues with them too. Therefore, you see it is very clear! We have a regional thing to deal with as we also seek to go further afield to remain an attractive business destination.

In addition, a final word of caution. Do not chase after flags when you have a sizeable market at home but do so if you must. The call is yours.

4

PROBLEMS OF SMALL BUSINESS ENTERPRISES

The big question: Why is it that in the financial marriage with banks the corporate companies take the "For better" part and the SMEs certainly the "for worse" part?

It is no doubt to all that the entire world experiences both recessions and boom swings. The resultant effects mean different things to all businesses today. Let us focus on one segment that is a buzzword only in good times. The SME[5] sector, it is widely argued, is or should be the driving force behind our economy. This fact therefore makes it obvious for the financial sector to give it great focus.

In times of recession, no financier is as loud about this sector as they are, in boom time, about why they provide the best solutions for the SME sector.

I however commend Government and IFC[6] efforts through various programs on renewed support to the sector and the efforts of FSD[7] that is finding innovative solutions for the sector.

Let us examine some reasons why this sector is openly embraced in boom times, and palmed off or out rightly ignored in bad times and provide some suggested solutions for the businessperson wanting to get back his footing.

Today the SME world means different things to different financial institutions. Some give it a bird's eye view while others give it a mole's eye view.

What one financial institution classifies as a medium sized business enterprise is classified as small business outfit by another institution. The opposite applies in smaller financial institutions when small business is classified as medium or big business.

It is through the lack of a uniform definition, in Kenya today that financiers find very wide gaps to structure products that favour them in boom times and allow them to retreat to unfamiliar solutions in times of recession.

The flipside of this approach by Financial institutions has led to SMEs being multi-banked to avoid putting all their eggs into the one basket that may leave them gasping in the wake of a policy shift or the fear of a bank collapsing.

The by-product of this is the perception that SMEs are not good depositors. Uniformity in classification of SMEs will allow for better choices on the part of borrowers as they will go for the closest fit. My view is that a generally agreed classification, be adopted across the entire financial system.

The SME world has one major challenge that their relatives in big business solved many years ago. Systems remain a major constrain to this sector. For the lender, this is an opportunity in boom time to price solutions at a premium and in times of recession an opportunity to term one as very risky and hence not a good option to support.

The savings anticipated in avoiding a good management system are deceitfully a costly mirage stemming from trusting that one's organization skills are adequate, and do not warrant the purchase a good system. In recent times, institutions such as the IFC and private software developers and dealers have availed suitable systems for SMEs. Sometimes entrepreneurs feel that they have outgrown learning the proper use of computers.

The SME sector in my view, unlike big business, lacks avenues to harness collective intelligence, an ingredient vital for use as a key player in the economy. Instead, they choose the lonely path paved with the curriculum that only ensures one ends up a graduate of the hard knocks institution of higher learning (gut feel approach) whose ultimate qualification is pain and wonder.

This has led to the lack of research on the part of entrepreneurs on such important elements as, profiting from the synergy of an effective small business association.

This body, will not only champion and lobby for their issues with government, but will also serve as a resource centre for issues such as effective branding, finding new markets, and to avoid the pit fall of being in a trade or business area that is already overcrowded, just to mention but a few.

Another harsh reality for SMEs is the fact that most of them never make it or come close to being in the list of say, twenty top customers of their financier, and who at all costs must be handled with care and given the "blood is thicker than water" attention and acceptance.

This very fact has its answer in joining for a bigger course. An observation in business is that the well organized, attract the orderlies that come in the form of experts, and financial institutions ready to listen to you when they sense a formidable critical mass.

Many SMEs, lack the skills required to put up winning proposals that can unlock credit from financial institutions. Even if they have good skills, in many instances, they lack the requisite records and documentation required to support these proposals. Getting a good financial consultant /advisor is critical for small business.

Again many SMEs unlike big businesses are not rated by independent rating companies and hence are difficult to assess and determine if safe or risky lending to. A number of them rely on management accounts as opposed to audited accounts hence making it hard to get a favourable opinion. It pays to have an official rating and a set of audited accounts.

Compounding from the points so far discussed, is the inevitable short-term memory syndrome that afflicts many SMEs that are always in fire fighting mode. This state usually emanates from lacking the elements that give you a position of strength as discussed above. Therefore, as you fire fight, you spread yourself thin, lose focus on the important issues, and wait for boom time to gain acceptance.

We also sometimes quickly forget the lessons learned in bad times and hence ensuring that we always get the 'for worse' part. Memory besides a good system requires excellent record keeping, diarizing of things to do and reviewing what is on record.

5

THE PITFALLS OF SMALL BUSINESS ENTERPRISES

The big question: What are the pitfalls that I must look out for in order to avoid getting into wasteful vicious cycles?

The first avoidable pitfall is the trap of products and services that fail to appeal to the market. How you introduce your products to the market is extremely critical given the vicious competition that has pervaded almost every existing sector.

Many businesses may be marketing finished products such as household goods or cars from the Far East. Others develop or manufacture services or tangible products respectively. Whatever your business, success will be measured by your product's acceptability via your target market's uptake.

There are people who use gut-feel as opposed to the tried and tested steps to product marketing.

Just to illustrate, a very gifted IT specialist set out to start what he believed would be an excellent business. He developed software for use in hospitals. This was a fully integrated system linking the back office, front office, accounts department and all other areas of the hospital operations. The system would seal all cash leakages and enhance efficiency.

Our friend moved from one hospital to another, marketing his wonder software but all in vain and to no avail. He soon abandoned his entrepreneurship quest and returned to gainful employment until the day a municipal official in his town stumbled across the software.

He liked it and purchased it, as it was just what was missing in the town's operations. It was perfect for towns and not hospitals. Very soon, other towns placed orders. So had he done his research well enough, he would have been in business from the get-go.

In summary, use the following approach to develop winning products. First, research thoroughly then incorporate the following Ps: Purpose of the product. Product design and features. Pricing the product in line with target market.

Promotion plan and Placement or distribution strategy. People who will provide the service or product to your market. Physical evidence if it is a service i.e. any physical thing related to the business, then a Positioning strategy and finally the Process(es) that will drive the business and deliver your product or service.

The second pitfall is that of cash flow. Just as every living thing has to eat to remain strong and alive, so is every business. Cash flow is the food that a business requires to grow up. Too little cash flow undermines overall performance of the business.

You must pay creditors, employees, service providers if you must remain in business and all these, are from your cash flows. You must understand your cash flows if you are to stand a chance to manage them.

If you are the marketing type that dislikes accounts, then stay out of business. To be in business you must be on top of every department.

Analyzing your cash flow needs is critical if you have to develop a cash flow budget. A cash flow budget will help you improve your cash flow and in turn enable your business to operate seamlessly.

Working at getting inflows faster than the outflows of cash from the business improves your overall cash position. With proper cash management, one can easily see when its right to borrow to finance operations or the opposite when you have surplus cash that can further improve your business.

Never spend from the business directly. Always do your banking regularly as this gives you traceability of real cash and overall, puts you in a good position to borrow from the bank if need be.

The third pitfall is that of the management team. If you are a sole proprietor, you must be good at all departments. You must be in a position to market and at the same time have financial capabilities.

No matter the size of business, people are the most important resource. You must understand the entire skills set required for your business so that you hire correctly at both the skill and knowledge level as well as the actual number of staff needed.

It is sometimes possible, to entirely rely on relatives but this only works for very few businesses, as most prefer to hire the best from the market.

You must be able to keep motivation levels high and keep improving your management skills. In many instances, your business will be just as good as your systems and employees. If you pay peanuts, expect to hire monkeys.

The final pitfall is the hardest of all. The business enterprise has grown; it is profitable and has developed a life of its own under good hands. The business owner has grown older but finds it very hard to hand over the button to the next person to manage. More so, if it is a family set up.

Many people, who preferred to take their children overseas for further studies, are finding it hard to get successors within the family to manage the business because the children settled abroad and find it difficult to come back to a third- world way of life.

In other instances, strange traditions mentored us to hide everything from the children until one-dropped dead. Then when picking the pieces together, curiosity turns into excitement and then the youngsters go on a spending spree until there is no more to spend.

A good succession plan is critical for the survival of any business. If your model allows, you can choose to introduce partners who over time take senior partner position. The other way is to sell it all together at a premium. Find the best plan for your business.

6

THE BANK

The big question: How do I identify a good bank, and what else do I need to know about banks?

For starters, in a well-regulated environment complete with prudential guidelines and stringent rules, the character or cultural practices of all banks within a jurisdiction become a see-through.

We are lucky to have come this far given that we have seen worse in the past. Because of big brother watching, the consumer is largely now left to concentrate on his or her bank of choice.

It is only obvious, that one must choose a bank that affords him the convenience of reach so that trips to the bank do not become a major event unless one is deliberately doubling up banking and physical exercise.

Many banks today have a presence in the major commercial centers and this is further boosted by the recent surge in branches countrywide. This brings convenience closer to all.

Secondly, how do you know the best bank? There is no straight answer to this if anything; there are as many answers to this as there are customers. This is so because, the best bank is determined by your own circumstances and incidentally that is where your needs emanate from. Let me advance this explanation with facts.

Banks build themselves around a strategy that makes them excellent at a certain service or set of services. The strategy determines what kind of systems to put in place and the resources necessary to enable it realize planned objectives.

To this end, you may complain that one bank's services are not as good as those that are provided by another simply because, you fail to appreciate that your requirements fit well elsewhere.

 In the market today, hardly any bank will willingly loose business by telling you that they are number five in what you are seeking and that it is best if you went down the road where number one is located. This applies to other industries too.

Business targets sometimes come on the way of strategy because, it is the numbers that one delivers that justify the yearend bonus. In short, get to know the core business of your prospect bank and see how it reflects against your core banking requirements.

Stemming from the above, are odd things we find ourselves doing. Some people ride on parental influence or sentimental attachments in choosing a bank without realizing that their fore bearers' circumstances are or were mutually exclusive.

Others get into fashion mode and find themselves cat walking with the crowds into banks that are not meant for them.

The simple rule, is know thy self. If you know your needs well enough, then you will know the kind of questions to ask and make your judgment.

Size of a bank and that of the customer, are both critical in choice. There could be a mismatch between customer and bank and the obvious, is the level of service that you get.

Much as many banks take a broad-spectrum approach to providing all rounded solutions for as many customers as possible, the word "core business" remains watermarked on all dealings and just need you to see through.

If you do not share a number of similar characteristics with the top say 100 customers not just in size, but also in the targeted attributes, then I am sure that you will complain as frequently as your favorite song keeps playing in your mind. Why walk your way into a boxing ring when you are actually a weight lifter?

The deals a bank can get into are partly influenced by its size, strategy, or both. For instance, a bank whose core capital is at the one billion shillings mark, cannot lend more than 25% or two hundred and fifty million shillings to any single borrower. Likewise, there are much bigger banks, when core capital is measured, whose strategies confine them to lending smaller amounts to a wider customer base as a way of spreading their risks.

In the two cases above, the possible scenarios are that of a customer moving away from a larger bank that lends smaller amounts, to a much smaller bank lending bigger amounts based on the 25% regulation, as is the case when one is transitioning from a micro business to a medium sized business.

The other way and usually is a customer outgrowing a smaller bank when the business graduates to a much bigger league where its needs are legally above the maximum applicable to the smaller bank. It is critical for you to right size and match yourself to your prospective bank so that you are within the purposed service actions of the institution.

Now with all the above, I hope that deciding on whom to bank with is simpler. Let me now focus on the extremely simple things that you must also do.

When you get a new chequebook, do you count all the leaves? A clever chap may tear off the last leaf at the back of the book and defraud you. Please ensure that in tandem with the physical leaf count; also look out for the progressive flow in the leaf numbering.

Never judge a book by its cover. I have come across several people who associate very expensive looking bank branches with the high and mighty especially in the rural setting.

Many people feel comfortable with familiar surroundings but when pitched above the norm, instead get cowed by a well intended spend on good looks. Going in to find out, does not cost a dime so feel free after all, you deserve better.

Your bank statements, are not "a nice to have" item. They are "a must have" item. Besides them coming in handy whenever you need credit, it is important to go through them carefully. There could be a mistake on the part of the bank that is easily corrected when it is pointed out.

On the shocking side of life, a dishonest bank employee could notice that you are ignorant and over time help you to spend your hard-earned money. Sometimes just asking questions about your account can be a good deterrent to theft.

Finally, I am not a lawyer but I do know that when you get into a joint loan facility either as husband and wife or as business partners in a venture, the term "**joint and several**" appears in the letter of offer.

This means, that in the event that the loan goes bad, the bank may pursue an obligation against any one party involved in the transaction for the full amount, even if your portion in the business is a paltry two percent, and your partner having the balance.

If, you are a two percent shareholder, but with easily attachable assets, that would give the bank its desired relief, then the bank, will find it attractive to attach your assets.

The bank may not go after the ninety-eight percent shareholder, if his assets are less desirable.

So be watchful as money matters can in equal measure cause or cost you a smile.

7

AN EXCELLENT PRODUCT

The big question: How do I get my product to be popular with my target market?

 You must recognize that the customer is part of your product definition.

You may have come across a very energetic and enterprising businessperson. The type, who identifies opportunities and moves fast, to cash in by introducing products that can satisfy his intended target market.

He has the speed whose reward comes from what in business is termed as "first-mover advantage". This is what makes companies be known as the first in a certain field and by extension become the market leader.

Now you may know someone with this level of energy and has hardly succeeded in making the difference that he had despite having had the first move advantage. A number of reasons could be responsible for this.

For starters, the entrepreneur could have enthusiastically overstocked to a point where he deprives himself of the liquidity needed to create the much-needed awareness of his products to the market.

In such a case, the customer remains in the dark and cannot be aware of the wonder products. The entrepreneur had the market benefits in mind but no plan to access the market.

Then, another opportunity savvy person gets his gap and grabs the market then uses the overstocked entrepreneur as a temporary merchandise warehouse. Could this be happening to you?

Secondly, a situation that is ubiquitous, is that where, products are not clearly defined and fail the positioning test in the prospective customer's mind. When you do not have it positioned in the customer's mind, then it has not yet become a product.

Let me use financial services to illustrate my point. Bankers are very acronym oriented in their conversations. This is fine if it is within the confines of the work environment but not when talking to customers.

Financial services are complex in nature especially to the average mind. The average mind constitutes the biggest market for any products. The sharpest minds constitute a fraction of the market and in most cases are the most critical of any offerings to the market. Were they the only ones in the market, then only the complex sounding products, could sell.

Now that we are on the same page on the fact that most consumers are either average in the knowledge of what they consume, or that they need to be aware of their existence, it only makes sense to develop products or services and present them in a manner that an average person can grasp their use or importance.

The banker is a technical person and on average, his target is in the dark only until he becomes aware of the service at hand. If a bank, came up with a product that aids companies, to both safely and conveniently disburse salaries to casual workers, and calls it "Bank Pay" with the acronym BP. It is only the employees of that bank that know this product inside out but, approaching a customer for business, the relationship person, may say we have BP to aid your management of casuals. Two possibilities come to mind.

One, you may be talking face to face with the kind of person who asks questions and would want to know more about BP. Even if the customer finally is bought-in, the selling process was stretched by unnecessary jargon.

Secondly, you may be talking face to face with the kind of person who does not ask questions and tags along to conceal his ignorance of the meaning of BP . In such a case, the transfer of the meaning of BP into the customer's mind is incomplete and what was otherwise simple, was left sounding complex to an average mind. The result, NO SELL.

There are many situations around us today that are related to this illustration. You could be one of those who find themselves, lost for words. The rule is, always start with the market penetration and awareness strategy before you develop or stock up your products.

Please remember that to succeed, win the customer's mind. To do so, make it as simple as possible. Simple means easy to understand. Why sell a **Three Wheeled Petrol Powered Town Maneuver Object (TWPPTMO)**, when what you actually mean is a tuk tuk? [8]

8

SELLING TO THE RICH

The big question: What do I need to keep in mind, when selling my products to rich customers?

There are three distinct groups of people that, I will describe so that we get a fair understanding of the word "rich". The cut-off point is high up the ladder.

First, there are those who appear rich because they have all the signs of the rich. E.g., they drive good cars, live in good neighbourhoods and socialize with the very wealthy but seldom do their bank accounts see the new money overlapping with old money at end month. In this case, old money is what you earned thirty days back. These are the aspiring.

Then you have those that exhibit much more affluence and have no cash flow problems unlike the first group. These are about to arrive.

Finally, you have those who are recession proof and get money coming in faster than it is spent. These are the "rich". These I assume are your target.

Now supposing your personal attributes do not fall anywhere within or close to the three categories, would you call all the above rich? I advise that you do not. In any case, I believe that you shall one day get there.

If you are already within this definition, then congratulations are in order! There are ways of analyzing and concluding on who is rich or not and this is your introduction to the top end. You must be keen. The genuinely rich, are often the cognitive elite of society. What they think and say goes.

When you are in this market segment, you come across those whose slogan is "fake it till you make it". These are the China eggs of your business pipeline. They never hatch but want to be associated with anyone giving attention to the rich. You must be keen enough to sift out this group and pack them in your "wrong target" bin.

Sometimes comparisons do not help. For instance, the richest man in a poor neighbourhood is not necessarily a rich person. I do not also mean that s/he is not your targeted prospect.

Similarly, the best-kept fence in a leafy neighbourhood is not a euphemism for wealthiest resident as it could be courtesy of a well-negotiated company paid package complete with the requisite blue-collar men. I will discuss later how I qualify a rich person.

Also, bear in mind, that there are rich and poor business people. Business just like human life has the top end and its paupers.

The well-to-do have worked their way to self-actualization and as a result, they occupy the highest tip of the pyramid, in Maslow's hierarchy of needs[9]. At this high point, the rules of accessing the rich change. For starters, the mass-market way of advertising is not effective as this group, is largely insulated, from the very many marketing efforts directed at them.

If you extended an event invite to a rich wo/man, chances are that the secretary/ PA would screen and only allow it through if it is of interest.

Therefore, anything about the rich is critical to you. The gardener, security guard and secretary are some of the gatekeepers that can make the difference. How you deal with them is critical. Is it not ironical that to access the rich, you must learn to manage the very modest people around them?

The wealthy, unlike the upcoming or the aspiring, are not "WANNA BEs." If anything, they are very collected most of the time, and will most likely prefer, to deal with either familiar products or familiar faces.

To have familiarity, you must have the time to know and hang out where they do. It is not always true that the rich only hang out in exclusive clubs. Often times, the richest people in a hang out are not necessarily the fanciest dressed, not the ones buying the most drinks or the ones driving the sleekest cars.

Occasionally, Rich businesspersons climb down on to the "ordinary" man's pedestal to scan and upload vital new realities from the environment. After all, the ordinary people supply businesses with the much-needed product consuming critical mass. After meeting with their suppliers and distributors earlier on, they make time to meet with their consumers albeit informally and that is where you come in.

Please note that the term "ordinary" means different things to different industries and firms of various sizes. The much respected management trainee at your hang out is ordinary in the eyes of the chairperson of a small security firm. Likewise, the security firm chairperson happens to be ordinary in the eyes of the assistant security manager in the big multinational that is tendering for security services.

Incognito appearances do not give away clues to the casual eye. Many times, the clue is in the conversations. They are always eager to learn from you without letting out excitement even on moneymaking ideas.

In an effort to contain your possible reduction to a self-responding questionnaire, engage by tactfully asking questions that guide your conclusions of the deep-pocketed target so that opinions are mutually shaped.

The free drinks coming your way could be used to categorize you as "having potential and also great for conversation", as a "Pay as You Extract Information Object" or some mild form of "corporate social responsibility" to ensure the safety of the moneyed visitor.

How you position yourself, is crucial and key in determining any further contact. Positions taken that are well meaning and postures assumed that are natural, could be misinterpreted to mean the opposite so your demeanour must not exude repulsive signals.

Most times, the questions they ask, are meant to help shape their opinions or perceptions from your ordinary world perspective and so, they cannot afford to engage in petty talk. Moreover, if they do, then your favourite joint could be a hide out, some sort of a rich man's vices paradise, a place to bask under the hear-nothing–see-nothing rays of the incognito sun.

The rule here, is pay attention to the long-term views held and do not be destructed by the short-term company around your target. Be wise by giving space perhaps after exchanging contacts.

The moneyed are good at money matters and as such, are not always looking for ways to spend their hard-earned money. At times, you do come across a flamboyant prospect or the extravagant type. Chances are they never made that money. Someone elsc did. So du not be destructed by such tendencies. Focus on the desired target. When dealing with the rich have your facts right and remain patient. This is a virtue appreciated by this market segment.

Be confident about what you are proposing. The only way to do so is to do your homework and to prepare adequately. Remember that your target group never made their money in a hurry. So why hurry yourself out of the deal?

The upper end is a quality sensitive market and as such, you must recognize that cheap is expensive and to them, expensive is not necessarily equal to quality. They know this all too well. This segment wants to pay the right price for the quality that you are offering.

To offer quality, you must be prepared to put in resources in terms of money and time. The affluent can tell and appreciate where time, creativity and the right amount of financial resources, were put to good use to get to the product targeted at them. In short, you must be prepared to spend the right amount of money to get money out of your target market.

You can increase your visibility by sponsoring events organized by big companies or by the rich as individuals. This way, your products stick out. Make use of technology. Having a website can enhance your visibility because remember that the secretary cannot screen the bosses internet interests.

Find a way of being useful to this segment. Volunteer your services at a high profile event. Remember this group more often than not, make decisions and expect others to implement. Be the one implementing. Get to know the interests of your prospect and come in as a solution provider. This way you catch the eye of your target.

Everyone whether rich or poor is human and as such negative tendencies such as nagging irritate. This is the last thing that you want to be associated with because this market is an endorsement market and word goes out fast.

Now how do I identify the affluent? I have a simple acronym used by sales people. **MAN** this stands for Money, Authority, and Need.

Be sure, that you are talking to the person with the **Money** and secondly has the **Authority** to spend that money. This could be authority to spend corporate money or an individual's own money.

With the first two pointers concluded, then there must be a compelling **Need** for your prospect to spend the money. In the absence of this, then it is your job to create the need and this is where excellent selling skills come into play.

If you are targeting the discerning type, then you are dealing with the MANE with the E standing in for **exposure**. Exposed customers, know what exactly they want and this can make all the difference if you are spot on.

9

BRANDING

The big question: What truths about branding should I keep in mind, when focusing on my business?

Employing proper business branding strategies could spell the success for your business. Although it might be an intangible aspect of your business, it is what convinces people to buy or avail of your products or services. Moreover, when you garner enough sales, then only then can your business thrive.

What is a Branding Strategy?

A brand is not just a logo or a name; it represents your business identity. Therefore, it is a crucial part of the start-up process for any business. Branding strategies are employed to provide the fundamental steps and recognize the valuable tools that will help create a strong business brand.

 In general terms, a strong brand is one that people recognize and believe to deliver good quality. Have you ever found yourself at the grocery choosing one product over the other because it is the more recognized or trusted brand?

It is therefore a branding strategy's objective to recognize what could turn your business into a trusted brand name. How can you make people trust your brand and its reputation? What should you do to communicate the objective and mission of your company? What is the message you are trying to send out to produce loyal customers? A sound business branding strategy will aim to find answers to these questions before you can establish a brand for your company that would excel in the market.

Create Name, Logo, or Website

Coming up with a name for your business goes hand in hand with creating a logo that will identify your company. When it comes to logos, always opt for something unique. Logos will be utilized in your advertising and marketing campaigns, so it must be well recognized.

For beginners, think of a logo that will readily hint consumers about the nature of your business – such as whether you are in the food, automotive, or telecommunications business. Hence, choose images that are associated with the nature of your business and the products they will be used to represent.

Slogan or Tagline

Once you have the logo that you want, you can think of a slogan that will reinforce the message you are trying to communicate to the consumers. As long as you keep this part brief and straightforward, then this can be an effective branding tool for your business. This tagline will serve as an additional touch to the main message you are trying to give, thus giving you an edge over your competitors and highlighting the unique experience or service that consumers will be able to avail of.

One advantage that you can get with including a tagline is that it is not permanent, unlike the logo. Therefore, if your company wishes to employ a new marketing strategy, you can readily change your tagline to highlight this new marketing ploy.

A tagline then opens up several opportunities to expand your marketing campaigns, as compared to the static nature of company logos because they are the ones more difficult to establish.

Colours and Images

As with logos, colours and images can be used to establish the identity of your business. Colours depict a corresponding set of emotions as well. Therefore, you need to carefully pick out exactly what type of colour you are going to use in your logo in accordance with the image and personality of your business. Try to conduct a little bit of research about the different qualities of colour types so you can determine exactly what best to use for your company.

Unique Services

When communicating your company brand into the market, highlight the services that only you can offer. If you can guarantee a service that none of your competition can, then you create an edge on your customers over the same businesses. Then, you can use that as a chief marketing strategy to draw more people into your business. An example of this would be a time guarantee on your delivery services, if you are in the food business.

Learning how to effectively employ these business-branding strategies will help boost your company's campaign and be that much closer to your desired business success.

Common Branding Mistakes and Myths to Avoid

What Makes a Brand Identity?

Branding is an aspect of every business that consist of visual elements that are used for the company's marketing purposes.

Therefore, most business owners would hire a professional logo designer to execute the concepts laid out by the company, which they believe will help communicate the company's business into the market. This logo will then be used as a marketing material that will appear on business cards, envelopes, letterheads, or other professionally related materials.

Establishing that brand identity is one of the initial steps that must be taken by a company if it wishes to achieve market success. Hence, this process must involve careful brand planning and though to avoid damaging your business. You must also look into how the customers might perceive the message being delivered by your brand, to avoid having it work against you.

Designing the Brand

There is no need to reiterate the importance of your brand identity to the success of your business. Therefore, this is an area of your business planning and start-up that must be left to the professionals, especially if you are new to the business industry.

Although you might have a sense of creativity, graphic designing becomes an entirely different concept when it is associated with using it as a marketing tool.

Apart from being creative and visually appealing, the brand logo must have meaning and is able to convey essential information about your company. Here are some benefits you can get from hiring a professional to design your logo:

The creation of your brand logo will serve as priority. Hence, you are able to set a specific time frame for the completion of the job to ensure that it is being focused on closely.

Customizing Brand Design

Contrary to popular belief, designing your own company logo to use as marketing material is not expensive. However, this is relative; especially if you insist on using high-quality materials for this but this is totally your own preference should you have a big budget for this. If not, then a sound concept and a skilled logo designer will be able to produce a strong brand.

After all, this is a business investment since your brand can affect your sales. This is a relatively inexpensive investment with a potential for a lucrative profit.

Understanding the Importance of Branding

Several businesspersons tend to neglect the creation of a brand identity. Therefore, most of them fail in their business endeavours and yet they do not even realize where the lapses are coming from. A brand identity is as essential as some of the basic priorities in every business start-up such as a business name, bank account, or operating system. Moreover, if ever a brand is created, most business owners do not look into the details of the brand and thus ending up with a brand that misrepresents their company.

Below is a list of common branding mistakes that must be avoided:

• Failure to create an efficient brand planning strategy

• Not giving full commitment to the management and review of the brand.

• Inability to establish internal branding.

• Lack of a sound marketing plan.

• Trying way too hard to create distinction to the point of inaccessibility.

Branding your business is never easy but once you recognize the factors that could impede your business' progress, then you are on your way there.

10

PERSONAL BRANDING

The big question: How important is personal branding and how do I go about it?

Personal branding has been defined as the process whereby people and their careers are marked as brands. Personal branding concept suggests that success comes from self-*packaging* a term thought to have been first used by Tom Peters. Nothing highlights the importance of this more than the emergence of branding services for CEO's to increase visibility and profits. If in doubt, just Google and be amazed at how many choices of these services you will find.

There is no doubt that if one is a good brand today, all the trappings that come with success stick better and come faster. The opposite leaves one stranded.

Many of us in business or in the work place at one time have had a moment of glory that today is just a story and not a horseback to ride on. You may have been at the top of your class consistently but today none of your classmates are around to turn this fact for you to a brand. Therefore, what you have is stranded success.

Let us examine what the distinctly branded people do and have in order to stand out on their own or with the aid of rare attributes that many wish to have or be associated with. This include, beauty, brains, physique, confidence etc

First, they stand for something that becomes strongly associated with them and hence get the credentials of consistency for this. Obama stood for change in the election campaigns and became a global phenomenon.

Many notable experts have a pet subject or project that makes them stand out. The key word is standing for something and not necessarily someone. If for instance one gets branded for always standing for the boss and nothing else, then you risk being stranded in the wake of his or her exit from the organization.

Secondly, is the use of, or attraction by publicity channels such as the print, electronic and now digital media. Publicity from such channels make one an instant figure of whatever magnitude the channels can reach.

Word of mouth is also an effective channel. Face book is a free channel of communication through which many people are becoming bigger brands. The same channels can leave one stranded when one looses credibility or when all the opposites come to the fore.

Successfully branded people, have the immense ability to embrace change and remain relevant with the times. One important attribute to have, is the ability to transcend today's opportunities by transmuting your "now" brand into a more permanent form. This is true for a member of the Kenya 7s rugby team (none of whom are professional players) and who right now has the potential of being branded a success when age and good form are on his side but risks going to oblivion when new and younger talent takes their place in the team.

In this case, the rugby player can use his present status on a first move advantage basis over the rivaling new talent, to grow into a long lasting brand by turning his competitiveness in the game to competitiveness in business or sports administration.

This is one attribute that every businessperson can single out. It will be easier for you to open doors of opportunity and generate business on the back of your "now" brand redirected. The sports legend of the '60s Kipchoge Keino[10] is a living example today of successful personal branding out of the track to international sports administrative duties that has kept his brand relevant.

Further, afield, Tyra Banks, cat walked her way from the fashion floor to her own television talk show and has maintained her visibility.

Confident brands reaffirm their credentials and authenticity among equals. This happens when one belongs to an association, professional body or grouping that adds value. There is no better publicity to get than what comes free from peers. These groupings also help one gain access to resources such as career enhancing materials, which in turn increase your confidence. Professionals in isolation have no wave to ride on.

All the attributes above, snow ball ones brand by attracting contacts and friends who help to keep the momentum going by becoming the much needed wave to ride and remain successful.

FOOT NOTES

1 Taken from Robert Kiyosaki's book "Rich Dad Poor Dad"

2.The Black Empowerment Program, is an equalization strategy of the Government to give employment opportunities to black citizens as a result of the earlier apartheid system that segregated blacks and favored whites.

3. Swahili is a language widely spoken in East Africa.

4. Amharic is one of the languages spoken in Ethiopia.

5.SME is the acronym for Small and Medium sized Enterprises.

6. IFC – International Finance Corporation

7. FSD – Financial Sector Deepening.

8.Tuk Tuk . A three wheeled petrol or diesel powered vehicle of low engine capacity. It was introduced to Kenya from Asia.

9. Maslow's Hierarchy of needs is a pyramid shaped categorization of human needs starting with the most basic such as clothing, food and shelter at the base, and esteem needs at the middle and self-actualization needs at the apex.

10. Kipchoge Keino. According to various media reports, this man is one of Kenya's greatest athletes of all time. He broke middle and long distance track records at the Olympic Games and remains an inspiration to young athletes.

ABOUT THE AUTHOR

David Mugun is a business mentor, speaker and author.

He has helped several SMEs with strategic and operational issues on the back of his experience in both the banking and insurance industries, where he held senior positions.

David is a member of the International Mentoring Association-IMA, Professional Coaches Mentors and Advisors -PCMA and Professional Trainers Association of Kenya-PTAK among others.

He lives in Nairobi with his family.

CONTACT DETAILS

DAVID MUGUN

P.O Box 35 -00621

NAIROBI

TEL: 254 (0)728 866605